Simple Business Expansion Guide:

Easy Steps for Growing Small Businesses

Victor M. Berta

copyright massage

Table of contents:

Why Expand?
CHAPTER 1
Get Ready:
    Is Your Business Ready?
CHAPTER 2
Plan Ahead:
    Make a Growth Plan
CHAPTER 3
Know Your Customers:
    Understand Who Buys
CHAPTER 4
Money Matters:
    Budget Wisely for Business Expansion
CHAPTER 5
Make It Run Smoothly:
    Running Your Business with Excellence
CHAPTER 6
Spread the Word:

The Power of Telling More People About Your Business

CHAPTER 7

Sell More:

Elevate Your Sales and Propel Business Growth

CHAPTER 8

Tech Help:

Leveraging Technology for Business Growth

CHAPTER 9

Facing Challenges:

Navigating Business Obstacles and Problem-Solving for Success

CHAPTER 10

Following Rules:

Upholding Standards and Doing Things Right in Business

CHAPTER 11

See How You're Doing:

Measure Your Progress

CHAPTER 12

Real Stories:

Extracting Valuable Lessons from

Business Experiences
The End (For Now)

Celebrate Your Growth and Prepare for What's Next

As you approach the culmination of this transformative journey, it's a pivotal moment to stop, reflect, and bask in the celebration of the growth you've achieved. The process of expansion you've started upon transcends mere strategies; it represents a profound metamorphosis that alters the trajectory of your business and propels your personal growth as an entrepreneur. In this closing chapter, we'll dig into the significance of commemorating your achievements, engage in introspection about the lessons garnered, and equip you for the forthcoming ventures as your business's journey of growth continues.

Introduction:

Why Expand?

In the dynamic realm of business, growth is more than a mere choice; it's an imperative. As the visionary founder or owner of a small business, you've nurtured the seed of an idea into a successful reality. The journey from conception to establishment has been an exhilarating one, marked by moments of success and lessons learned. Yet, as you stand at this point, a pivotal question arises: "Why expand?"

The thought of steering your business beyond its current horizons may appear daunting, but it's a query that every entrepreneur must face. This chapter goes on a journey to unearth the reasons that elevate business growth from a possibility to an undeniable opportunity.

1. Embracing New Horizons:

Business expansion shows an expansive canvas of fresh possibilities. It propels you into uncharted territories and shows your goods to novel markets and demographics. In an interconnected global landscape, growth stretches far beyond the boundaries of local operations. By broadening your reach, you tap into a wider customer base, forging new income streams that breathe life into your business.

2. The Power of Economies of Scale:

The very act of expansion often ushers in the age of economies of scale. As your business grows, so does your capacity to create more with reduced costs per unit. This inherent efficiency boost translates into elevated profitability, allowing you to offer competitive prices while safeguarding healthy profit margins.

3. Mitigating Risk through Diversification:

Pinning your business's fate solely on one product or market can be a precarious venture. Expansion serves as a protection against this risk. By diversifying your product line and entering fresh markets, you insulate your business from the reverberations of market volatility. A downturn in one area exerts minimal effect on your overall operations.

4. Crafting a Resolute Brand Identity:

Crafting an indelible brand identity is an art, one that growth magnifies. Venturing into uncharted areas catapults your business into the spotlight of a larger audience. This heightened exposure turbocharges brand recognition, bolstering your stance in a fiercely competitive field.

5. Seizing the Competitive Edge:

The business arena lives on dynamism and rivalry. Expansion presents a rare chance to outpace competitors by establishing a presence in new markets ahead of them. This head start on the competitive circuit solidifies your footing and helps the capture of coveted market shares.

6. Attracting the Best and the Brightest:

Business growth unfurls a welcoming mat for the crème de la crème of ability. Flourishing businesses exude innovation and advancement, rendering them a magnet for top-tier professionals wanting a platform to shine.

7. Riding the Waves of Trends:

Industries unfurl along the tapestry of evolving trends and shifting customer inclinations. Expansion equips your business to pivot and handle these transformations, ensuring that you stay relevant and well-poised to cater to the evolving needs of your patrons.

8. Cultivating a Culture of Innovation:

Expansion rejuvenates your business's creative instincts. The novel challenges met in uncharted markets breed innovation as you seek ingenious solutions. This infusion of novel views breathes new life into your strategies and approach.

9. Personal and Professional Growth:

Business expansion isn't solely about the growth of your business; it's a conduit for your personal evolution. The triumphs and tribulations of expansion crystallise into invaluable experiences that add to your growth as a visionary entrepreneur.

10. Ensuring the Legacy of Your Enterprise:

Expansion isn't just a present-day choice; it's an investment in the future. By broadening income streams and fortifying your market positioning, you're not merely ensuring profitability today, but securing the longevity and sustainability of your business in the years to come.

In the forthcoming chapters, we'll explore these compelling reasons in intricate detail. Whether your gaze is set on unexplored markets, diversification of your product offerings, or forging ahead of competitors, this guide will serve as your compass through uncharted territory. As we start on this odyssey of business growth, we'll unearth the untapped potential that lies just beyond the horizon you've come to know.

CHAPTER 1

Get Ready:

Is Your Business Ready?

In the world of business, expansion isn't simply a vault of faith; it's a strictly planned trip that requires careful study and medication. Before you set passage into new requests or start innovative product lines, you must ask yourself a question: Is your business ready? This vital question is further than a checkpoint; it's a critical tone- assessment that can determine the success of your growth sweats. In this chapter, we'll explore the crucial factors that indicate your business's readiness for growth and accompany you through the process of assessing your business's strengths and areas that might need underpinning.

Assessing Current Performance

Before charting a course for expansion, take a close look at your business's present performance. Are your deals harmonious and showing signs of growth? Is there a desire for your product or service that extends beyond your current reach? Strong and harmonious success is a solid foundation for expansion. It indicates that your business has formerly sculpted a space in the request and has the implicit to thrive in new regions.

functional effectiveness

Smooth operations are the backbone of any business.However, it's a good sign that your business can handle the fresh demands that come with growth, If your current operations are streamlined and effective. estimate your product styles, force chain operation, and client service to insure they're robust enough to handle increased volume.

Financial Stability

Expansion frequently needs a fiscal investment. It's important to assess your business's fiscal health before taking this step. Do you have the necessary cash to fund the expansion without compromising your current operations? Are your cash inflow and profit rates stable? A financially stable business is better set to ride the challenges that expansion might bring.

Strong Leadership and Team

Your business is only as strong as the platoon behind it. estimate the leadership within your company. Do you have an able operation platoon that can handle the difficulties of expansion? Are your workers aligned with your business's things and values? A strong and cohesive platoon will play a vital part in successfully navigating the growth process.

Understanding request Demand

Expansion should be driven by request desire. Is there a clear desire for your product or service in the new requests you are considering? Conduct thorough request study to understand the requirements and preferences of your implicit guests. This information will guide your expansion strategy and help you conform your immolations to reverberate with the new followership.

Adaptable Business Model

An adaptable business model is important for expansion. Can your current business model be gauged or modified to fit the demands of new requests? Inflexibility is crucial, as growth frequently comes with unlooked-for challenges and openings. A business model that can be tweaked to fit different request conditions is more likely to succeed.

structure and coffers

estimate your business's structure and tools. Do you have the physical and technological means to support expansion? This includes everything from manufacturing installations to IT tools. spanning up without the necessary tools in place can lead to functional backups.

Brand and Character

Your brand's image is a precious asset. Consider how your business is perceived in the current request. Is it well- regarded? Does it connect with your target followership? Expanding with a strong brand image can give you a head start in gaining the trust of new guests.

Risk Management

Expansion comes with natural pitfalls. estimate your threat operation tactics and contingency plans. Are you prepared to handle unanticipated challenges that might appear during expansion?

A robust threat operation system can minimise implicit risks.

Cultural and Regulatory Considerations

Entering new requests frequently means navigating artistic differences and varying laws. Are you set to acclimatise your business practices to misbehave with original rules and customs? An amenability to learn and admire the nuances of new requests is important for successful expansion.

client Feedback and fidelity

What do your present guests say about your business? Positive client feedback and strong fidelity are pointers that your business is offering value. Consider seeking feedback from your current guests on your expansion plans. Their perceptivity can give precious advice.

In conclusion, the question" Is your business ready?" isn't a clear yes or no. It takes a comprehensive evaluation of colourful aspects of your business. Each of these factors adds to your business's readiness for expansion. Before embarking on this transformative trip, take the time to assess your business's strengths, sins, and possible areas for enhancement. Armed with this information, you can make informed opinions that set the stage for a successful expansion. Flash back, readiness is not just about meeting the criteria; it's about setting your business up for growth and substance in the new midair you are about to discover.

CHAPTER 2

Plan Ahead:

Make a Growth Plan

Expanding a small business is akin to going on a thrilling voyage—one brimming with new prospects and heightened achievements. Yet, as the adage wisely tells us, "Failing to plan is planning to fail." When it comes to the ambitious endeavour of business expansion, the cornerstone of success lies in a meticulously structured growth plan. This isn't just a paper; it's the strategic blueprint that charts your course to success. It paints the path, pinpoints the resources, and lays out the strategies needed to realize your expansion aspirations. Within this chapter, we'll plumb the depths of the growth plan's significance and delve into its pivotal components, propelling you toward your development aspirations.

The Significance of a Growth Plan:

A growth plan takes the role of your compass, steering you unerringly toward your goal while allowing the flexibility needed to manage the dynamic business landscape. In its absence, expansion efforts can scatter, choices might meander sans coherence, and resources could be squandered. Here's why a growth plan is indispensable:

1. Clarity of Direction and Focus:

A growth plan sets forth a crystal-clear trajectory for your development voyage. It outlines the endgame, strategies, and objectives, ensuring every stakeholder grasps the final destination and the roadmap that leads there. This laser focus thwarts distractions and keeps the alignment of your team.

2. Optimal Resource Deployment:

The expansion engine wants resources—financial, human, and operational. A growth plan is your guide to carefully allocate these resources. By discerning what's required and when it's needed, you orchestrate a symphony of resource utilization, sidestepping wasteful extravagance.

3. Taming the Risk Beast:

Expansion is joined by an entourage of risks, and a growth plan empowers you to predict and pacify these perils. By identifying potential hurdles and outlining contingency plans, you're ready to face unforeseen challenges with grace.

4. Progress Tracking and Accountability:

The growth plan seeds measurable goals and success benchmarks. This enables progress tracking, where your team is held accountable for achieving milestones. Regular evaluations identify deviations from the plan, urging timely course corrections.

5. Cultivating Investor Confidence:

Should your expansion quest involve external funding, an impeccably drafted growth plan is a prized tool. Investors seek concrete assurance that your endeavour is underpinned by a tangible plan, ready to reap returns. A robust plan instils investor trust and draws potential backers.

Components of a Growth Plan:

Crafting a growth plan demands a meticulous examination of multifarious facets that contribute to expansion's completion. While particulars fluctuate based on industry and business specifics, here's the crux of the important components for your growth plan:

1. Executive Summary:

A succinct primer to your growth plan, encapsulating your business's current state, developmental goals, and strategic undertakings.

2. Business Analysis: A thorough dissection of your business's strengths, weaknesses, opportunities, and threats (SWOT analysis). This bedrock offers a foundation for your expansion strategies.

3. Expansion Goals and Objectives:

Lay out your growth goals lucidly. Are you entering virgin areas, diversifying your product bouquet, or swelling your market pie? This section enunciates Specific, Measurable, Achievable, Relevant, and Time-bound (SMART) goals.

4. Market Exploration:

Voyage into uncharted markets through meticulous study. Understand the target demographic, market dimensions, competition, and customer behaviors. These findings form the bedrock of your marketing and sales game plans.

5. Marketing and Sales Manoeuvres:

Unveil how your goods or services will be ushered into these fresh areas. This includes your pricing strategy, distribution avenues, and promotional tactics.

6. Financial Forecasts:

Project revenues, expenditures, and profits over a set timeline. These figures cast a realistic light on your expansion's financial feasibility.

7. Operational Orchestration:

Architect a plan for scaling your operations to meet burgeoning demands. Consider factors like production capacity, supply chain efficiency, and logistical acumen.

8. People and Prowess Strategy:

Delineate the human resources needed to anchor your expansion voyage. Expound on hiring roadmaps, training endeavors, and measures to retain your current talent pool.

9. Tech Infusion and Infrastructure:

Assess the technological requisites of your growth. Ascertain whether systems need upgrading, tools require acquisition, or your digital footprint warrants improvement.

10. Risk Roping: Cognizant of potential pitfalls and challenges entwined with growth, craft contingency strategies delineating how you'll navigate if these challenges morph into reality.

11. Timeline and Milestone Etchings:

Devise a timeline that chronicles pivotal events and their deadlines. This blueprint confers a structured timetable for your expansion efforts.

12. Monitor and Evaluate:

Lay the groundwork for tracking progress and judging the success of your growth plan. Anchor success standards and earmark junctures for periodic review.

13. Financial Allocations and Funding:

Estimate the monetary outlay necessitated by growth, inclusive of marketing costs, operational outflows, and supplementary investments. Determining the financial pulse to fund these efforts is important.

In summation, a growth plan is more than ink on paper; it's the strategic tool fueling your expedition through the labyrinthine corridors of business growth. Through the blueprint of a comprehensive growth plan, you galvanise your progress, channel resources judiciously, and face obstacles with preemptive insight. Remember, a growth plan lives on evolution; it adapts as your business flourishes and new vistas beckon. Armed with a meticulously crafted growth plan, you're ready to unfurl the sails, starting on the next phase of your expansion odyssey, fortified by a compass that unfailingly guides you toward victory.

CHAPTER 3

Know Your Customers:

Understand Who Buys

In the realm of business, knowing your customers is akin to possessing a treasure map that leads to success. It's a fundamental principle that can guide your choices, drive your strategies, and shape your offerings. As you embark on the journey of business expansion, this principle becomes even more important. The ability to truly know your customers—beyond superficial demographics—can be the key to opening new markets and maximising growth. In this chapter, we'll explore the significance of understanding who buys from you, dive into the art of customer segmentation, and uncover the strategies that can help you make stronger connections with your audience.

Why Understanding Your Customers Matters:

Customers are the heart of any business. The better you understand their needs, preferences, and behaviours, the more effectively you can tailor your goods or services to meet those needs. This understanding goes beyond knowing their age, gender, and location; it involves delving into their motivations, challenges, and aspirations. Here's why truly knowing your customers is paramount, especially when expanding your business:

1. Targeted Marketing:

Imagine having a chat with a friend who understands your thoughts and feelings. Similarly, knowing your customers allows you to speak directly to their pain points and desires through your marketing efforts. This targeted method resonates more deeply and leads to higher engagement.

2. Tailored Offerings:

Expanding your business might involve introducing new goods or services. By understanding your customers, you can develop offers that meet their specific needs, increasing the chances of success in new markets.

3. Building Trust:

When people feel understood, they are more likely to trust your brand. Trust is a cornerstone of customer loyalty, and loyal customers are more likely to follow you into new markets or recommend your business to others.

4. Entering New Markets:

Expanding often means entering new markets with varied customer behaviours and preferences. Understanding these nuances helps you adapt your strategies and offerings to fit the unique needs of each market.

5. Minimising Risks:

Expanding without a deep understanding of your customers can be risky. Your expansion efforts may not align with what your target audience actually wants, leading to possible failures. Understanding your customers minimises this risk.

Strategies for Understanding Your Customers:

1. Customer Segmentation:

Customer segmentation includes dividing your customer base into distinct groups based on shared characteristics. This can include demographics (age, gender, location), psychographics (lifestyle, values), and behavioural traits (purchase history, contact with your brand). Segmentation allows you to tailor your marketing efforts to each group's unique needs.

2. Data Analytics:

Harness the power of data to gain insights into customer habits. Analyse data from sources like website traffic, social media interaction, and purchase history. Tools and platforms exist to help you make sense of this data and discover trends that inform your strategies.

3. Surveys and Feedback:

Directly asking your customers for opinion is invaluable. Surveys, feedback forms, and social media polls can provide insights into their tastes, pain points, and expectations. Use this knowledge to shape your offerings and strategies.

4. Social Listening:

Monitor social media platforms and online communities to gauge customer sentiment and discussions about your brand. This real-time feedback can help you spot emerging trends and adapt your approach accordingly.

5. Customer Interviews:

Engage in one-on-one interviews with a sample of your buyers. This qualitative method offers deeper insights into their motivations, challenges, and perceptions.

6. Competitor Analysis:

Studying your rivals can offer insights into their customer base and strategies. Identify what works for them and adapt those tactics to fit your brand and target group.

7. Continuous Engagement:

Customer preferences change over time. Regularly connect with your audience through social media, email newsletters, and interactive content to stay updated on their changing needs and desires.

8. Empathy and Listening:

True knowledge comes from empathy and active listening. Put yourself in your customers' shoes, and seek to truly comprehend their experiences and perspectives.

9. Persona Creation:

Create customer personas—fictional characters representing different segments of your community. These personas serve as a reference point for crafting marketing messages and making strategic choices.

In conclusion, the art of knowing your customers is an ongoing journey that takes continuous effort and a genuine commitment to empathy. As you expand your business, this understanding becomes even more crucial, as it helps you to connect with diverse audiences and adapt to new markets. Remember, knowing your customers isn't just a business tactic; it's a relationship-building effort that fosters loyalty, trust, and ultimately, sustainable growth. By knowing who buys from you, you're not only unlocking the treasure trove of customer insights but also the doors to untapped chances in the world of business expansion.

CHAPTER 4

Money Matters:

Budget Wisely for Business Expansion

Expanding a business is a thrilling journey that holds the promise of increased income, a wider customer base, and enhanced brand recognition. However, the road to expansion is paved with financial considerations that can greatly impact the success of your endeavour. In the world of business, wise budgeting is not just a good practice; it's an important strategy for navigating the complexities of growth. In this chapter, we'll delve into the realm of financial planning for business growth, emphasising the importance of budgeting carefully and providing insights into effective budgeting strategies.

The Role of Budgeting in Business Expansion:

Budgeting is more than just crunching numbers; it's a strategic tool that leads your financial choices and allocates resources for optimal results. When it comes to business growth, a well-crafted budget can provide the following benefits:

1. Financial Clarity:

A budget offers a clear snapshot of your financial resources and responsibilities. It helps you understand how much capital you have available and how it can be allocated across different parts of your expansion.

2. Resource Allocation:

Business expansion needs resources, including capital, manpower, and operational assets. A budget helps you allocate these resources efficiently, stopping overextension in one area while neglecting others.

3. Risk Mitigation:

Expansion is followed by risks. A budget allows you to set aside contingency funds for unforeseen challenges, minimising the effect of unexpected hurdles.

4. Measurement and Accountability:

A budget sets measurable cash goals. Tracking your real expenses against the budgeted amounts provides a clear gauge of your progress and keeps your team accountable.

5. Investor Confidence:

If seeking external funding, a well-documented budget instils confidence in prospective investors. It shows that you've fully considered the financial aspects of your expansion and are prepared to manage resources wisely.

Effective Budgeting Strategies:

1. Assess Your Current Finances:
Before expanding, take stock of your current financial position. Evaluate your revenues, costs, cash flow, and profit margins. This baseline knowledge informs your budgeting decisions.

2. Define Your Expansion Costs:
Clearly identify the costs involved with your expansion efforts. This includes not only direct expenses like marketing and operations but also indirect costs that might come from increased demand or production.

3. Create Realistic Revenue Projections:
Estimate the additional revenue your expansion is expected to create. Be conservative in your estimates to avoid overestimating income and underestimating costs.

4. Prioritise Expenses:

Not all costs are equal. Prioritise your expenses based on their effect on your expansion goals. Allocate more resources to areas that directly add to growth and customer acquisition.

5. Build in a Contingency Fund:

Plan for the unexpected by allocating a part of your budget to a contingency fund. This safety net can cushion the effect of unforeseen challenges or changes in the market.

6. Research Funding Options:

If your expansion needs additional capital, explore various funding options. This might include loans, investors, crowdfunding, or reinvesting gains. Choose the choice that aligns with your business's financial goals and risk tolerance.

7. Monitor and Adjust:

A budget is a dynamic tool that needs ongoing monitoring and adjustment. Regularly compare your real expenses with your budgeted amounts and make necessary adjustments as circumstances change.

8. Embrace Flexibility:

Business growth is accompanied by uncertainties. Your budget should be flexible enough to handle unexpected changes or shifts in the market landscape.

9. Involve Your Team:

Your team's feedback is invaluable when crafting a budget. Involve key stakeholders from various departments to ensure that the budget reflects the reality of your business activities.

10. Invest in Growth:

Allocate funds to areas that directly contribute to growth, such as marketing, product development, and growing your team. Strategic investments can yield large returns in the long run.

11. Track Return on Investment (ROI):

As you perform your expansion strategies, track the ROI for each investment. This data will help you refine your strategies and utilise resources more effectively in the future.

In conclusion, budgeting carefully is not just about managing money; it's about strategically stewarding your business's financial resources to achieve your expansion goals. By assessing your financial health, estimating costs, and prioritising expenses, you're setting the stage for a successful growth that is financially sustainable and strategically sound. Remember, budgeting isn't a one-time job; it's an ongoing process that requires vigilance and adaptability. With a well-structured budget in hand, you're prepared to start on your expansion journey with confidence, knowing that your financial base is strong and your resources are allocated to maximise growth potential.

CHAPTER 5

Make It Run Smoothly:

Running Your Business with Excellence

As you start on the journey of business expansion, envision a well-oiled machine that effortlessly navigates the complexities of growth. The foundation of a successful expansion rests on your ability to run your business easily and efficiently. From optimising processes to fostering a positive work culture, every facet of your business plays a role in ensuring that expansion is not just a dream but a reality. In this chapter, we'll explore the art of running your business well, emphasising the strategies and principles that contribute to a seamless growth experience.

The Importance of Running Your Business Smoothly:

Running a business smoothly is more than just a matter of convenience; it's a strategic necessity. When you run your business efficiently and effectively, several benefits emerge that directly impact your expansion efforts:

1. Scalability:

A business that runs smoothly is naturally scalable. Streamlined processes, clear communication, and efficient routines are the building blocks of scalability. As you grow, these elements allow you to replicate successful operations in new markets.

2. Customer Satisfaction:

Smooth processes translate to better customer experiences. When customers receive goods or services promptly and seamlessly, their satisfaction increases, fostering brand loyalty and positive word-of-mouth.

3. Resource Optimization:

Efficient processes result in optimised resource allocation. This means you can achieve more with the same tools, whether it's your workforce, equipment, or finances.

4. Employee Engagement:

A well-run business gives employees with the tools, processes, and support they need to excel in their roles. This promotes a feeling of engagement and satisfaction, which translates to increased productivity and reduced turnover.

*15. Adaptability to Change:

Change is expected, especially during expansion. A business with smooth operations is better able to adapt to new challenges and opportunities, ensuring that growth doesn't disrupt day-to-day activities.

Strategies for Running Your Business Well:

1. Streamline Processes:

Identify bottlenecks, redundancies, and flaws in your business processes. Streamline processes to minimise unnecessary steps and optimise resource utilisation.

2. Invest in Technology:

Embrace technology that improves efficiency. This might include workflow tools, project management software, and customer relationship management (CRM) systems.

3. Clear Communication:

Effective communication is the backbone of smooth processes. Ensure that information flows seamlessly among different departments and levels of your company.

4. Empower Your Team:

Provide your team with the resources, training, and autonomy they need to succeed. Empowered workers are more likely to take ownership of their roles and contribute to the business's success.

5. Monitor Key Performance Indicators (KPIs):

Define KPIs that align with your business goals. Regularly monitor these metrics to track your business's success and find areas for improvement.

6. Customer-Centric Approach:

Prioritise your customers in all your activities. Align your processes and strategies with the goal of providing exceptional value and experiences to your customers.

7. Continuous Improvement:

Adopt an attitude of continuous improvement. Encourage your team to spot areas for enhancement and provide suggestions for refining processes.

8. Efficient Supply Chain Management:

If your business involves physical products, optimise your supply line. Timely procurement, effective inventory control, and reliable suppliers add to smooth operations.

9. Flexibility in Leadership:

Be open to adjusting your leadership style based on circumstances. Flexibility allows you to change your management style to different situations and employee needs.

10. Encourage Collaboration:

Foster a collaborative setting where different departments and teams work together cohesively. Cross-functional collaboration can lead to innovative ideas and smoother operations.

11. Employee Training and Development:

Invest in training programs that enhance your workers' skills. Well-trained employees are more confident and capable of adding to your business's success.

12. Focus on Quality:

Consistently delivering high-quality goods or services is a hallmark of a well-run business. Quality builds trust with buyers and sets you apart from competitors.

13. Delegate Effectively:

Delegate tasks to the appropriate individuals based on their skills and expertise. Effective delegation prevents burnout and ensures chores are handled efficiently.

In conclusion, running your business well is an ongoing effort that requires dedication, strategy, and a drive to excellence. When you create an environment of efficiency, clear communication, and continuous improvement, you're not just setting the stage for a smooth expansion; you're also laying the groundwork for sustained success in the long run. Remember, running your business smoothly isn't just a goal; it's a dynamic process that changes with your business and adapts to new challenges and opportunities. With a focus on running your business well, you're able to handle the demands of expansion while keeping a solid foundation of operational excellence.

CHAPTER 6

Spread the Word:

The Power of Telling More People About Your Business

At the heart of every great business lies the ability to sell successfully. Increasing sales isn't just about pushing goods or services; it's about knowing your customers, meeting their wants, and creating value that resonates. As you start on the journey of business growth, the goal of selling more becomes even more crucial. It's not just about generating income; it's about fueling growth, expanding your customer base, and solidifying your place in new markets. In this chapter, we'll explore the strategies that can help you sell more, improve your sales efforts, and drive your business towards steady growth.

The Significance of Selling More:
Selling more isn't solely a pursuit of wealth; it's a strategic imperative for business growth. Consider the following reasons why growing your sales is important, especially during times of growth:

1. Revenue Generation: Increased sales simply lead to higher income. This income fuels your business's growth efforts, from entering new markets to investing in product development.

2. Market Penetration:

Expanding your business needs a bigger customer base. Selling more allows you to enter new markets and reach customers you might not have addressed before.

3. Competitive Edge: A business that regularly sells more gets a competitive advantage. It positions itself as a market leader and sets a high bar for rivals to match.

4. Scaling Efforts:

As you expand, your business processes need to scale as well. Increased sales provide the resources needed to support growth without reducing quality or customer experience.

5. business Visibility: The more you sell, the more your business becomes noticeable. Increased sales efforts show your business to a

bigger audience and strengthen brand recognition.

Effective Strategies to Sell More:

1. Understand Your Customer's Needs:
Before you can sell more, you need to understand what your customers truly need. Conduct thorough market study to find pain points, desires, and preferences.

2. Tailor Your Offerings:
Customise your goods or services to meet unique customer needs. Offering personalised solutions improves the chances of getting a sale.

3. Provide Exceptional Value:
Focus on giving value that goes beyond the product itself. Solve problems, address pain points, and offer solutions that enrich your customers' lives.

4. Offer Bundles and Upsells:

Encourage buyers to purchase more by giving bundles or upsells. This adds value to their buy and improves your average transaction value.

5. Improve Customer Experience:
A seamless and enjoyable customer experience leads to repeat business and suggestions. Invest in customer service, easy purchasing ways, and post-purchase support.

6. Leverage Social Proof: Positive reviews, testimonials, and case studies provide social proof that your goods or services give results. Showcase these to build trust and reliability.

7. Create Scarcity and Urgency: Limited-time offers, flash sales, and exclusive deals create a sense of urgency that pushes customers to make a purchase sooner.

8. Implement Cross-Selling and Up-Selling:
Cross-selling involves suggesting complementary goods, while up-selling involves

giving higher-end alternatives. Both methods improve the value of each sale.

9. Invest in Sales Training: Equip your sales team with successful training. This includes product knowledge, objection handling, and effective communication skills.

10. Build Relationships: Focus on building ties with your customers rather than just making a sale. Long-term ties lead to repeat business and company loyalty.

11. Targeted Marketing: Utilise data to segment your group and build targeted marketing campaigns. This ensures that your word gets the right people with the right offer.

12. Provide Educational Content: Share educational content that demonstrates your expertise and gives value to your group. This places your business as a trusted resource.

13. Offer promises: Provide promises that remove the risk for buyers. A satisfaction guarantee or money-back offer improves their confidence in making a buy.

14. Create a reward Program: Reward regular customers with a reward program. This incentivizes them to make more purchases and supports brand loyalty.

15. Optimise Pricing Strategy:
Price your things or services strategically. Test different price methods to find the one that maximises sales and profit margins.

16. Embrace E-Commerce and Online Platforms: If possible, spread your business to online platforms. E-commerce opens up new paths for sales and allows you to reach a global audience.

17. Continuous Innovation: Keep your goods or services fresh and useful by continuously innovating. New offerings draw attention and entice current customers to make repeat purchases.

18. Monitor and Analyze Data:

Regularly examine sales data to spot trends, customer behaviours, and areas for improvement. Data-driven ideas guide your sales tactics.

19. Provide Outstanding After-Sales help:

Post-purchase help and follow-up improve the customer experience. Address any issues quickly and go the extra mile to ensure customer happiness.

20. Measure Return on Investment (ROI):

Evaluate the success of your sales efforts by measuring ROI. This helps you discover which strategies are offering the most value.

Principles for Successful Sales Efforts:

1. Customer-Centric Approach: Focus on fulfilling customer wants rather than pushing goods. A customer-centric way builds trust and loyalty.

2. Listen and Adapt: Listen to customer feedback and adapt your sales methods properly. Flexibility ensures you're meeting changing customer standards.

3. Transparency and Honesty:
Be open in your sales attempts. Honesty builds trust, which is important for repeat business and recommendations.

4. Consistency: Consistency in your message and customer interactions reinforces your brand personality and builds trust.

5. Focus on Value, Not Price:
Emphasise the value your goods or services provide rather than competing simply on price. Value-based selling supports higher price points.

In conclusion, the ability to sell more is a critical skill that underpins the success of any business, especially during times of growth. By implementing effective strategies, understanding your customers' wants, and focusing on giving value, you're positioning your business for growth and success in new markets. Remember, selling more is not just about transactions; it's about building relationships, making good experiences, and driving your business towards sustained wealth. With a strategic approach to growing sales, you're not only achieving revenue goals; you're also nurturing a foundation of customer loyalty and market impact that goes far beyond the realms of your present operations.

CHAPTER 7

Sell More:

Elevate Your Sales and Propel Business Growth

At the heart of great businesses lies a mastery of effective selling. Amplifying sales transcends mere product promotion; it involves understanding customers, catering to their needs, and cultivating value that resonates deeply. As you start on the odyssey of business expansion, the pursuit of selling more takes paramount significance. It's not a mere income generator; it's a catalyst for growth, a key to broadening your clientele, and a cornerstone in asserting your position in new markets. In this chapter, we're set to explore the strategies that unlock the door to selling more, infuse dynamism into your sales endeavours, and navigate your business toward a trajectory of steadfast growth.

The Essence of Selling More:
The goal of selling more isn't a singular dance with profitability; it's a strategic mandate for business growth. Delve into the following reasons that spotlight the import of growing your sales, especially in times of expansion:

1. Revenue Amplification:

Elevated sales usually usher in greater financial inflow. This monetary influx fortifies your growth initiatives—be it market entry or product creation.

2. Penetrating Fresh Markets:

Expanding needs an expanded customer base. Selling more unfurls the chance to venture into uncharted markets and seize the attention of untapped patrons.

3. Competitive Prowess:

Businesses that perpetually push the limit in sales ascend the competitive echelons. They carve their niche as market trailblazers, setting benchmarks competitors aim to match.

4. Enabling Seamless Scaling:

Expansion demands that business machinery grows in tandem. Enhanced sales funnel resources toward seamless growth, sans reducing quality or client experience.

5. Elevation of Brand Presence: With each transaction, your brand shines brighter. Elevated sales efforts spotlight your business before a broader audience, imprinting brand memory ever more deeply.

Strategies to Augment Sales:

1. Decode Customer Needs:

Embark on the journey of selling more by decoding what customers truly desire. Through comprehensive market study, unearth pain points, cravings, and preferences.

2. Tailor Your Offerings: Calibrate your goods or services to cater to unique customer demands. Personalised solutions bolster the likelihood of landing a sale.

3. Deliver Exemplary Value:

Shift the spotlight from goods to value that transcends the transaction. Solve quandaries, alleviate concerns, and offer solutions that improve the lives of your patrons.

4. Bundles and Upsells: Empower customers to elevate their buying experience through bundles and upsells. This augments the value of their buy and lifts your average transaction value.

5. Elevate Customer Experience:
A seamless, gratifying customer experience forges customer loyalty and word-of-mouth recommendations. Invest in customer service, hassle-free purchase journeys, and post-sales help.

6. Harness Social Proof: Positive reviews, compelling testimonials, and success stories give social validation to your offerings. Harness these to build trust and credibility.

7. Invoke Scarcity and Urgency:
Infuse your sales efforts with a sense of urgency via limited-time offers, flash sales, and exclusive deals, compelling customers to act swiftly.

8. Integrate Cross-Selling and Up-Selling:

Cross-selling suggests complementary products, while up-selling gives superior alternatives. Both strategies amplify the value of each buy.

9. Cultivate Sales Proficiency: Empower your sales squad with effective training. This includes product mastery, objection handling, and polished communication finesse.

10. Cultivate Relationships: Forge bonds with customers beyond the deal. Long-term relationships end in repeat business and unwavering brand loyalty.

11. Laser-Sharp Marketing:
Leverage data to segment your audience and create targeted marketing endeavours. This ensures your message reaches the right audience with apt offers.

12. Dispense Educational Content: Disseminate educational content that showcases your expertise and imparts worth. This positions your business as a trusted information hub.

13. Extend promises: Extend promises that obliterate risk. A satisfaction guarantee or refund pledge bolsters customers' confidence to make a purchase.

14. Institute Loyalty Programs: Extend rewards to faithful customers via a loyalty program. This stimulates recurrent purchases and cements brand loyalty.

15. Strategize Pricing: Strategically price your products. Experiment with various pricing models to discover the one that maximises sales while preserving profit margins.

16. Embrace E-Commerce and Online Platforms: Consider an online business growth through e-commerce. This opens avenues for sales expansion and gives access to a global clientele.

17. Perpetual Innovation: Continuously infuse innovation into your services. Novel products captivate attention and entice current customers to return.

18. Scrutinise and Analyze Data:

Regularly dissect sales data to spot trends, customer behaviours, and avenues for improvement. Insights gained from data chart your sales trajectory.

19. Stellar Post-Sales help: Post-purchase help and follow-ups amplify the customer experience. Swift resolution of problems and exceeding expectations nurture satisfaction.

20. Gauge Return on Investment (ROI):

Evaluate the efficacy of your sales efforts by scrutinising ROI. This unveils the strategies that give the most value.

Principles for Sales Excellence:

1. Customer-Centricity: Prioritise fulfilling customer needs over peddling goods. A

customer-centric ethos promotes trust and lasting loyalty.

2. Listen and Evolve:

Listen attentively to customer comments and adapt sales strategies accordingly. Flexibility ensures you stay aligned with evolving customer expectations.

3. Transparency and Integrity:

Embed openness in sales efforts. Honesty lays the basis of trust, crucial for enduring customer relationships and referrals.

4. Consistency: Maintain consistency across messages and customer interactions. This reinforces company identity and nurtures trust.

5. Emphasis on Value, Not Cost: Emphasise the value your goods bestow, transcending mere price comparison. Value-based selling bolsters the viability of higher price points.

In summation, the art of selling more is a cardinal skill underpinning the success of any

business, especially in expansion efforts. By embracing strategic strategies, empathizing with customer needs, and proffering value, you position your business for growth and success in novel domains. Selling more isn't confined to transactions; it's about fostering connections, nurturing good experiences, and steering your business toward enduring wealth. With a well-orchestrated strategy to fortify sales, you're not solely accomplishing revenue goals; you're nurturing a foundation of unwavering customer devotion and market clout that goes beyond your present horizons.

CHAPTER 8

Tech Help:

Leveraging Technology for Business Growth

In the dynamic world of business, technology isn't just a convenience; it's a driving force that can propel your company to new heights. As you set out on the road of business expansion, harnessing technology becomes paramount. From optimising processes to connecting with a global audience, technology offers a myriad of tools and strategies that can redefine your business's direction. This chapter explores the significance of utilising technology for growth and explains practical ways to make the most of it.

The Role of Technology in Business Expansion:

In the context of business growth, technology acts as a catalyst that accelerates your efforts. Here's why embracing technology is a game-changer:

1. Streamlined Operations: Technology automates tasks, slashes manual mistakes, and boosts efficiency. By integrating technology, you can scale processes while maintaining quality.

2. Data-Driven Insights:

The digital realm produces a wealth of data. Using technology to analyze this data gives you insights that inform your expansion plans, enhancing decision-making.

3. Extended Reach:
Thanks to the internet, geographical borders blur. Embracing technology allows you to reach a global audience, opening doors to new markets.

4.   Enhanced   Customer   Experience:
Technology helps you to understand your customers better, tailoring experiences to their preferences. From personalized marketing to smooth online shopping, tech elevates customer encounters.

5. Agility and Adaptability:
Innovation is key in a rapidly changing market. By embracing technology, your business can quickly adapt to changing conditions, keeping you ahead of rivals.

Practical Strategies for Effective Tech Adoption:

1. Digital Marketing:

Utilise digital marketing methods like SEO, content creation, and social media advertising. Targeting digital platforms expands your brand's visibility and connects you with a bigger community.

2. E-Commerce Platforms:

If feasible, create an online store. E-commerce simplifies transactions for customers and paves the way for global sales possibilities.

3. Customer Relationship Management (CRM) Software:

Integrate CRM software to manage customer interactions, track leads, and improve relationships. This technology consolidates customer data, allowing personalized engagement.

4. Process Automation: Identify repetitive jobs that can be automated. Automating jobs such as inventory management and order processing frees up valuable resources.

5. Data Analytics:
Invest in data analytics tools to extract useful insights from your business data. Analyzing customer behavior and market trends informs your growth strategies.

6. Cloud Computing: Leverage cloud computing for data storage and access. Cloud technology supports collaboration among remote teams and offers scalability.

7. Customer Support Solutions: Implement online support solutions like robots. These technologies provide immediate help and improve the customer experience.

8. Mobile Optimization: Ensure your website is mobile-friendly. With the rise of smartphones, mobile optimization ensures a smooth user experience.

9. Virtual Reality (VR) and Augmented Reality (AR): Consider using VR and AR to improve customer experiences. These immersive technologies are impactful in businesses like real estate and retail.

10. Cybersecurity Measures:
Prioritise cybersecurity to safeguard data and keep customer trust. Implement firewalls, encryption, and safe authentication.

11. Remote Work Tools: Provide remote work tools for your team, allowing effective collaboration regardless of location.

12. Stay Updated and Innovate: Monitor technological advancements relevant to your business. Adopt emerging technologies that fit with your expansion goals.

Key Principles for Successful Tech Adoption:

1. Alignment with Business Goals:
Integrate technology that supports your business goals. Technology should be an effective enabler, not a distraction.

2. Scalability: Choose technology that can grow with your business. Scalable solutions accommodate increased needs seamlessly.

3. User-Centric Design: Prioritise technologies that improve user experiences for customers and employees alike.

4. Integration Capability: Select technologies that can easily integrate with existing systems. Integration avoids data silos.

5. Flexibility and Adaptability:
Be open to changing your technology stack as needed. Flexibility ensures relevance and success.

6. Data Privacy and Compliance: Prioritise data privacy and adhere to laws. Protecting customer information is important.

7. Continuous Learning and Training: Invest in training to ensure your team can effectively use technology. Learning increases the benefits of tech adoption.

8. Thoughtful Implementation:
Introduce technology gently and thoughtfully. Piloting new technologies helps assess their effect.

In conclusion, technology is a potent tool that can reshape your business growth. By leveraging technology, you're not only optimizing processes but also fostering creativity and enhancing customer experiences. Technology is more than a tool; it's a strategic enabler that equips you to navigate the complexities of growth and seize chances in the digital era. With a well-informed approach to technology adoption, you're empowering your business with the tools needed to thrive, innovate, and excel in an ever-evolving environment.

CHAPTER 9

Facing Challenges:

Navigating Business Obstacles and Problem-Solving for Success

In the realm of business expansion, challenges are not roadblocks; they are chances for growth and learning. The way to success is seldom smooth, and encountering obstacles is an inherent part of the journey. The ability to face challenges head-on and effectively solve problems is what separates successful businesses from those that falter. As you start on the adventure of business expansion, getting the significance of challenges and honing your problem-solving skills becomes paramount. In this chapter, we'll study the nature of challenges, the art of problem-solving, and the principles that guide businesses toward overcoming hurdles and achieving success.

The Significance of Facing Challenges:
Challenges are not setbacks; they are catalysts for growth and creativity. Embracing challenges during business growth offers several invaluable benefits:

1. Personal and Professional Growth:

Overcoming challenges takes adaptability, resilience, and learning. These experiences add to your personal and professional growth as a business leader.

2. Enhanced Problem-Solving Skills:
Challenges give opportunities to develop and refine your problem-solving skills. The ability to find creative solutions is a hallmark of great entrepreneurs.

3. Increased Resilience:
Resilience is the ability to bounce back from losses stronger than before. Facing and overcoming obstacles builds your business's resilience.

4. Innovation and Creativity:
Challenges demand thinking outside the box. They spark innovation and drive you to create new strategies and approaches.

5. Competitive Advantage:

Businesses that successfully address challenges gain a competitive advantage. Adapting to changing conditions places you ahead of less adaptable competitors.

Strategies for Effective Problem-Solving:

1. Define the Problem:

Before you can solve a problem, you must clearly describe it. Identify the root reason and understand the implications of the challenge you're facing.

2. Gather Information:

Collect relevant data, information, and insights conncctcd to the problem. Informed decision-making is based on a thorough understanding of the situation.

3. Analyse and Brainstorm:

Break down the problem into its components and analyse each part. Brainstorm possible solutions, encouraging creativity and diverse views.

4. Prioritise Solutions:

Not all options are equal. Prioritise options based on feasibility, potential effect, and alignment with your business's values and goals.

5. Test and Iterate:

Implement the chosen answer on a smaller scale to assess its effectiveness. If necessary, iterate and refine the answer based on real-world feedback.

6. Seek Expert Advice:

Don't hesitate to seek advice from mentors, advisors, or experts in relevant areas. Their experience can provide useful insights and alternative viewpoints.

7. Encourage Collaboration:

Involve your team in problem-solving. Diverse perspectives can lead to comprehensive solutions and create a sense of ownership.

8. Embrace Failure as a Learning Opportunity:

Not all solutions will work. View failures as chances to learn, adjust, and refine your approach.

9. Maintain a Positive Mindset:

A positive mindset creates resilience. Believe that obstacles are surmountable and that solutions can be found.

10. Continuous Learning:

Problem-solving is an ongoing skill. Stay updated on industry trends, gather new information, and change your strategies as needed.

Principles for Effective Problem-Solving:

1. Calm Under Pressure:

Maintain composure when meeting challenges. Clear thinking and rational decision-making are important during critical moments.

2. Open-Mindedness:

Be open to considering unconventional ideas. The best method might not always be the most obvious one.

3. Adaptability:

Flexibility is key in problem-solving. Be prepared to adjust your strategies based on new information or changing situations.

4. Data-Driven Decision-Making:

Base your solutions on facts and evidence whenever possible. Data-driven decisions are more likely to give positive results.

5. Ownership and Accountability:

Take ownership of problems and their solutions. Hold yourself accountable for the results, whether they are successes or lessons learned.

6. Long-Term Vision:

While addressing immediate challenges is important, consider the long-term implications of your answers. Strive for sustainable results.

7. Effective Communication:

Keep stakeholders informed about the issue and the steps you're taking to address it. Transparent dialogue builds trust and alignment.

8. Patience and Persistence:

Some challenges take time to settle. Be patient and persistent in your efforts, and don't give up soon.

9. Continuous Improvement:

Reflect on the success of your solutions and seek ways to improve. Constantly refine your problem-solving method based on feedback and results.

In conclusion, facing challenges and successfully solving problems are integral aspects of business growth. Instead of viewing challenges as obstacles, embrace them as chances to learn, innovate, and grow. By adopting strategic problem-solving approaches and developing a resilient mindset, you're not only navigating the complexities of growth but also building a foundation of adaptability that will serve your business well in the long term. Remember, challenges are not setbacks; they are stepping stones that lead you closer to your goals, foster growth, and push your business towards sustainable success.

CHAPTER 10

Following Rules:

Upholding Standards and Doing Things Right in Business

In the intricate dance of the business world, adhering to rules and conducting oneself with ethics isn't merely a matter of compliance; it's a fundamental cornerstone of success. The basis of any reputable and flourishing business rests upon ethical conduct, adherence to regulations, and an unwavering commitment to excellence. As you navigate the intricate journey of business growth, the significance of following the rules and doing things right becomes even more obvious. In this chapter, we'll dig into the gravity of upholding standards, the advantages of ethical behaviour, and the guiding principles that steer businesses toward sustainable victory through principled actions.

The Importance of Following Rules:

Rules, whether they stem from industry laws or internal guidelines, serve a vital purpose. Adhering to these rules carries several compelling reasons during the growth of your business:

1. Legal and Regulatory Compliance:

Staying within the bounds of rules ensures that your business works within the legal framework set by regulations. Avoiding legal complications is key for unhindered growth.

2. Reputation and Trust: Businesses known for ethical behaviour and rule following gain the trust of customers, partners, and stakeholders. A solid image is an invaluable asset.

3. Long-Term Viability:
Doing things right sets the foundation for sustained success. Ethical practices and adherence to rules lessen the risk of setbacks that could hinder your growth trajectory.

4. Competitive Edge: Companies consistently abiding by rules and keeping high standards stand out in the market. This differentiation gives a competitive advantage.

5. Employee Well-being and Loyalty:
A work environment that values ethical behaviour and rule adherence creates a positive

culture. Employees are more likely to stay loyal to a company that upholds its principles.

Benefits of Ethical Conduct and Doing Things Right:

1. Trust and Credibility: Ethical behaviour nurtures trust among customers, investors, and partners. It sets your business as dependable and credible.

2. Favourable Customer Perception:
Customers are more likely to support companies with strong ethical values. Ethical behaviour improves your brand's appeal and cultivates customer loyalty.

3. Robust Relationships:
Ethical behaviour adds to stronger relationships with stakeholders. Partnerships based on trust and shared values are more likely to yield mutual benefits.

4. Mitigated Risk: Adhering to rules and ethical standards reduces the risk of legal disputes, bad publicity, and financial losses.

5. Employee Satisfaction:
A workplace that upholds high standards attracts and retains ethical workers. Such people are more likely to align with your business's goals.

6. Nurtured Innovation and Creativity:
An ethical business culture encourages employees to think innovatively and add to the company's growth.

Strategies for Upholding Standards and Doing Things Right:

1. Establish Clear Guidelines:
Set forth unequivocal policies and guidelines that describe expected behaviour and standards. These provide a reference for workers and stakeholders.

2. Foster Education and Training:

Deliver ongoing training on rules, laws, and ethical behaviour. Well-informed employees are better equipped to make sound choices.

3. Lead Through Example: Leadership plays a key role in setting the ethical tone. Demonstrate a steadfast resolve to doing things right through your actions.

4. Encourage Reporting:
Foster a setting where workers feel comfortable reporting ethical concerns or rule violations. Respond quickly to such reports.

5. Implement an Ethical Decision-Making Framework: Develop a framework for responsible decision-making. This equips workers to navigate complicated situations while upholding ethical standards.

6. Conduct Routine Audits and Compliance Checks:

Regularly check compliance with rules and regulations. This proactive method prevents violations and allows for timely corrections.

7. Promote Open Communication:

Cultivate open channels of communication where employees can voice concerns or seek clarification about rules and ethical issues.

8. Infuse Ethics into Performance Metrics:

Consider incorporating ethical behaviour as a component of job ratings. This reinforces the value of adhering to standards.

9. Align with Industry Norms:

Stay updated on business best practices and standards. Aligning with these benchmarks improves your business's credibility.

10. Specify Consequences for Violations:

Clearly explain the consequences of rule violations or ethical breaches. Consistently enforcing penalties reinforces the value of compliance.

Principles for Doing Things Right:

1. Uphold Integrity:
Practice integrity in all efforts. Make ethical choices even when there's no one to watch them.

2. Prioritise Transparency: Transparency develops trust. Be open about your work practices and choices.

3. Embrace Accountability: Assume responsibility for your actions and choices. This shows your commitment to ethical conduct.

4. Pursue Continuous Improvement:
Strive for ongoing improvement in ethical practices and rule adherence. Be open to adaptation and refinement based on feedback and results.

5. Cultivate Empathy and Respect:
Treat workers, customers, and stakeholders with empathy and respect.

Ethical behaviour stretches to how you treat others.

6. Adopt a Long-Term Perspective: Make decisions with a focus on long-term effect. Doing things right often means sacrificing short-term gains for sustained triumph.

7. Embrace Flexible Ethics:
Recognize that ethical rules may need adjustments based on national, legal, or industry-specific contexts. Be adaptable while upholding key ethical values.

8. Encourage Collaboration and Seek Feedback: Collaborate with employees, stakeholders, and experts to ensure your ethical practices align with diverse views.

In conclusion, the act of following rules and conducting oneself with integrity isn't merely a procedural duty; it's a mindset that steers businesses toward enduring success. By upholding ethical standards, complying with laws, and making principled choices, you're not just propelling your business toward a path of integrity but also fostering trust, loyalty, and credibility. Remember, doing things right is an ongoing journey that necessitates vigilance, dedication, and a sincere commitment to ethical behaviour. With an unyielding commitment to upholding standards, you're cultivating a culture of excellence that not only fuels your business growth but also leaves a positive legacy in your industry, among stakeholders, and in the larger world.

CHAPTER 11

See How You're Doing:

Measure Your Progress

See How You're Doing: The Importance of Measuring Progress for Business Expansion

In the dynamic world of business growth, the old word holds true" What gets measured gcts managed." Measuring progress is not just a way to track performance; it's an introductory strategy for success. As your business navigates the complications of growth, knowing how to assess your progress and make data- driven opinions becomes essential. In this chapter, we'll claw into the significance of measuring progress, explore the benefits of data- driven perceptivity, and uncover the principles that guide businesses toward effectively tracking their trip of growth.

The Significance of Measuring Progress

Measuring success serves as a nautical tool that guides your business expansion trip. Consider the following reasons why tracking progress is pivotal

1. Clear Direction

Measuring progress gives a clear sense of direction. It helps you understand where you're in relation to your pretensions and whether you are on track.

2. Responsibility

Quantifiable data holds your business responsible. It's a palpable way to assess whether you are meeting the pretensions you've set.

3. Informed Decision- Making Data- driven perceptivity allows informed decision- timber. With accurate information, you can change strategies, allocate coffers, and prioritise sweats successfully.

4. Beforehand Problem Identification
Measuring progress helps you to identify challenges beforehand. This visionary system allows you to address issues before they escalate.

5. provocation and Focus Progress tracking provides a sense of success and encourages brigades to stay focused on achieving their pretensions.

6. Rigidity Real- time progress dimension allows quick adaptations to strategies. It's a flexible system that supports nimble decision- timber.

Benefits of Data- Driven perceptivity

1. Objective Assessment Data- driven perceptivity gives an objective view of your business's success. feelings and impulses are reduced, leading to more accurate assessments.

2. Fact- Grounded Decision- Making

rather than counting on suspicion alone, data- driven perceptivity gives concrete substantiation to back opinions.

3. Performance Benchmarking

Data allows you to standardise your performance against assiduity norms and stylish practices, relating places for enhancement.

4. Resource Allocation With data on hand, you can distribute coffers more effectively. This avoids destruction and optimises resource utilisation.

5. Threat Mitigation Data- driven perceptivity allows you to identify and alleviate pitfalls. It's easier to prepare for possible challenges when you are fortified with accurate knowledge.

6. nonstop enhancement Data analysis attendants nonstop enhancement attempts. You can spot patterns, trends, and areas where adaptations are demanded.

Strategies for Measuring Progress

1. Set Clear pretensions

Establish clear, measurable, attainable, applicable, and time- bound(SMART) pretensions. Clear pretensions serve as marks for growth.

2. Identify crucial Performance pointers(KPIs)

Define KPIs that match with your pretensions. KPIs give quantifiable criteria that represent your business's performance.

3. Regular Data Collection apply systems to collect important data regularly. This data gives the foundation for progress assessment.

4. Utilise Technology influences technology and tools to automate data collection and analysis. Technology streamlines the process and lowers crimes.

5. Track Financial Metrics

Fiscal pointers similar to profit growth, profit perimeters, and return on investment are important measures of progress.

6. client Metrics Track client satisfaction, retention rates, and feedback to assess the impact of your growth on your client base.

7. functional effectiveness

Examiner functional measures similar as product effectiveness, force chain performance, and force development.

8. Employee Engagement and Productivity

Assess staff satisfaction, productivity situations, and retention rates. Engaged workers add to your business's success.

9. request Share and Penetration

Measure your request share and how well you are piercing new areas. These criteria represent your business's growth line.

10. contender Analysis

Cover your challengers' performance to gain perceptivity into assiduity trends and implicit areas for growth.

11. client Acquisition Cost(CAC)

estimate the cost of gaining new guests. This metric helps you assess the effectiveness of your marketing and deals conditioning.

12. Return on Investment(ROI)

Measure the return on investment for different expansion enterprises. ROI shows the profitability of your expansion strategies.

13. client Continuance Value(CLV) Assess the value a client brings to your business over their continuance. CLV informs your marketing and client retention tactics.

14. Website and Social Media Analytics
use web analytics and social media criteria to gauge online engagement and the success of your digital presence.

Principles for Effective Progress dimension

1. Data Quality ensures the variety and trustability of your data. Inaccurate data can lead to deceived choices.

2. thickness
Maintain thickness in data gathering and dimension styles. harmonious data allows accurate comparisons.

3. Practicable perceptivity Data should give perceptivity that drives action. Avoid gathering data for the sake of it; concentrate on information that informs decision- timber.

4. Contextual Understanding Understand the environment behind your data. Interpretation needs sapience into the broader business geography.

5. Rigidity: Be ready to acclimate your criteria and pretensions as your business evolves. The capability to acclimatise ensures your measures stay applicable.

6. Long- Term Perspective
Measure progress with a long- term view. Short-term oscillations may not duly reflect your overall line.

In conclusion, measuring success is the compass that guides your business expansion trip. By setting clear pretensions, relating crucial criteria , and using data- driven perceptivity, you are not only tracking your performance but also perfecting your capability to make informed opinions. Flash back, success dimension is not just a shot in time; it's a nonstop process that requires alert, analysis, and rigidity. With a strategic approach to measuring progress, you are situating your business for sustainable growth, aligning your sweats with your pretensions, and icing that every step you take on the road of expansion is deliberate, informed, and eventually effective.

CHAPTER 12

Real Stories:

Extracting Valuable Lessons from Business Experiences

In the tapestry of business, real stories are the threads that weave together lessons, insights, and motivation. Learning from the experiences of others is a powerful strategy for success, especially when starting on the complex journey of business expansion. Real stories offer a glimpse into the challenges faced, the strategies employed, and the triumphs gained by entrepreneurs who have walked a similar road. In this chapter, we'll explore the significance of learning from real stories, the benefits of drawing insights from others' experiences, and the principles that guide businesses toward extracting valuable lessons for their own growth endeavours.

The Significance of Learning from Real Stories:

Real stories provide a bridge between theory and reality. They offer a firsthand account of the challenges, strategies, and results that entrepreneurs meet during their expansion journeys. Here's why learning from real stories is crucial:

1. Practical Insights:

Real stories offer real insights that textbooks and manuals can't copy. These insights are born from actual experiences and carry a depth of knowledge.

2. Learning from Mistakes:

Mistakes made by others can serve as warning tales. Learning from these mistakes helps you avoid similar pitfalls in your own expansion efforts.

3. Inspiration and Motivation:

Hearing about the successes made by others can be incredibly motivating. Real stories motivate you to persevere, innovate, and dream big.

4. Contextual Understanding: Real stories provide context for the decisions and strategies applied by entrepreneurs. You gain a better understanding of the circumstances that shaped their choices.

5. Emotional link: Real stories evoke an emotional link. They humanise the challenges and successes of business, making them relatable on a personal level.

Benefits of Drawing Insights from Others' Experiences:

1. Shortened Learning Curve: Learning from others' experiences increases your learning curve. You gain from their insights without having to go through the same trials.

2. Well-Rounded Perspective:

Real stories expose you to a diverse range of situations. This broadens your viewpoint and helps you anticipate various scenarios.

3. Strategic Decision-Making:

Insights from real stories help in strategic decision-making. You can make more informed choices by drawing parallels to similar conditions.

4. Risk Mitigation:

Learning from the challenges others have faced allows you to effectively mitigate risks. You can anticipate potential issues and plan properly.

5. Innovation and Adaptation:

By understanding how entrepreneurs adapted and innovated, you're inspired to do the same in your growth journey.

Strategies for Extracting Valuable Lessons:

1. Read Biographies and Autobiographies:

Biographies and autobiographies of great entrepreneurs provide deep insights into their experiences, decisions, and growth trajectories.

2. Attend Seminars and Workshops:

Participate in seminars, workshops, and group talks where entrepreneurs share their stories. These events offer firsthand accounts.

3. Listen to Podcasts and Interviews:

Podcasts and interviews provide a convenient way to listen to entrepreneurs narrate their experiences and thoughts.

4. Join Networking Events:
Networking events promote conversations with fellow entrepreneurs. Hearing their stories in person can be incredibly revealing.

5. Read Case Studies:
Case studies analyse real business scenarios, offering a thorough breakdown of the challenges faced and the strategies employed.

6. Engage in Online Communities:
Online forums and communities help entrepreneurs to share their experiences and advice. Engaging in these spaces offers a wealth of insights.

7. Seek Mentorship:
Mentors who have navigated business expansion can offer personalised advice and share their experiences directly.

8. Collaborate with Peers:

Peers who are on a similar expansion journey can share real-time thoughts and experiences that resonate with your challenges.

Principles for Extracting Valuable Lessons:

1. Open-Mindedness:

Approach real stories with an open mind. Be receptive to different views and strategies.

2. Contextual Application:

While drawing insights, consider how the lessons apply to your unique business situation. Adaptation is key.

3. Critical Analysis: Analyse the challenges and strategies given in real stories. Evaluate how those findings align with your own expansion plans.

4. Continuous Learning: Keep finding new real stories and experiences to learn from. The business landscape evolves, and there's always more to learn.

5. Humility:

Recognize that every entrepreneur's journey is special. While you can learn from others, you'll also chart your own way.

6. Balance of Perspectives:

Seek a balance between success stories and reports of challenges. Both provide valuable insights that add to a holistic view.

7. Adaptation and Innovation:

Use real stories as a source of motivation for adaptation and innovation. Apply lessons creatively to fit your expansion goals.

In conclusion, learning from real stories is a treasure trove of wisdom that enriches your business growth journey. By embracing the experiences of others, you're not only benefiting from their insights but also weaving a tapestry of knowledge that guides your own choices and strategies. Remember, real stories are more than anecdotes; they are a source of inspiration, guidance, and reassurance that you're not alone in your search for growth. With a commitment to learning from others, you're tapping into a reservoir of collective knowledge that propels your business forward, equipping you to overcome challenges, take opportunities, and write your own success story of growth.

The End (For Now)

Celebrate Your Growth and Prepare for What's Next

As you approach the culmination of this transformative journey, it's a pivotal moment to stop, reflect, and bask in the celebration of the growth you've achieved. The process of expansion you've started upon transcends mere strategies; it represents a profound metamorphosis that alters the trajectory of your business and propels your personal growth as an entrepreneur. In this closing chapter, we'll dig into the significance of commemorating your achievements, engage in introspection about the lessons garnered, and equip you for the forthcoming ventures as your business's journey of growth continues.

Celebrating Your Growth:

Amidst the whirlwind of business growth, it's imperative to carve out a moment to revel in your achievements. Celebrations serve as more than mere praise; they ignite a renewed zeal for the path ahead. Here's why recognising your growth is indispensable:

1. Acknowledgement of Endeavor:

Celebrations are a tribute to the toil both you and your team have put in the expansion process. Acknowledging hard work boosts confidence and self-assurance.

2. Impetus and Inspiration:

Commemorating milestones and triumphs acts as a wellspring of inspiration. It kindles the impetus to set fresh goals and stretch your limits.

3. Strengthening Bonds:

Celebrations create a sense of camaraderie within your team. It's a juncture to unite, honour each other's efforts, and nurture stronger relationships.

4. Reflection and Perspective:

Celebrations provide an interlude for reflection. It permits you to glance backward and appreciate the distance you've traversed, bestowing a broader perspective on your journey.

5. Fanning Future Momentum:

The euphoric ambiance made by celebrations propels you ahead. It instils zest and dynamism into your ongoing efforts.

Reflecting on Lessons Learned:

As one chapter closes, another begins. Devote time to ruminate on the insights you've gleaned during the odyssey of business growth. Reflection wields profound power for growth and change. Ponder over the following aspects:

1. Triumphs of Effectiveness:
Discern the strategies, decisions, and undertakings that bore good fruit. These form your strengths that can be harnessed in the days to come.

2. Overcoming Hurdles:
Meditate upon the challenges faced and your strategies for surmounting them. What wisdom did these experiences bestow, and how did they add to your evolution?

3. Areas Awaiting Refinement:

Foster candid contemplation about aspects that deserve enhancement. Reflect on what could have been executed differently and how these lessons can steer your future endeavours.

4. Personal Maturation: Reflect on your development as an entrepreneur through the growth trajectory. What proficiencies have burgeoned, and how have you changed as a leader?

5. Dynamics of Team Harmony:

Contemplate how your team engaged, communicated, and supported each other. Which team factors bolstered your successes?

Preparing for What's Next:

The termination of one part inaugurates the inception of another. As you bask in the glory of your successes and ruminate on your journey, it's imperative to brace for what awaits. Here are guidelines to think as you transition into the subsequent phase of your business's growth:

1. Envision Novel Objectives:

In tandem with your business's metamorphosis, fashion fresh goals that align with your plan for the future. Conceive lucid goals that kindle enthusiasm in your team and expedite progress.

2. Uninterrupted Quest for Knowledge:

The journey of growth is ceaseless. Pledge to perceptual learning and augmentation to stay at the vanguard of industry trends and innovations.

3. Embrace Adaptability and Flexibility:

The business environment is a perpetual flux. Cultivate the agility to adapt and the flexibility to face new prospects and surmount challenges.

4. Amplify Your Network:

Networking stands as an important resource for expansion. Forge alliances with peers, mentors, and experts to glean varied views and insights.

5. Empower Your Team: Your team takes an indispensable role in your business's ascendancy. Foster their empowerment by affording paths for growth and validating their contributions.

6. Pioneering Innovation and Experimentation:

Innovation represents the soul of expansion. Foster a culture of experimentation and creativity to uncover novel strategies and approaches.

7. Embrace the Flux of Transformation:

Change is the true essence of business. Confront change with an open spirit, recognizing it as a prospect to grow and enhance.

8. Regulate Regular Reflection:

Infuse periodic reflection into your routine. Consistent self-evaluation ensures alignment with your aspirations and enables adaptations to your strategies.

9. Remain Anchored to Your Vision:

 Amidst the unfurling of your business, cling to your basic principles and vision. These guiding tenets furnish direction and a feeling of purpose.

10. Rejoice in Milestones:

 As you achieve fresh milestones, commemorate them. Commemorating achievements maintains the momentum and creates a milieu of positivity.

In summation, the culmination of this expedition is the genesis of a new part of your business's growth. As you toast to your accomplishments, meditate on your learned lessons, and brace for the impending chapter, remember that every stride you've taken has added to the evolution of your business. Embrace the perpetual circle of growth, adaptation, and ingenuity. Though this chapter may end "for now," your odyssey as an entrepreneur and your business's odyssey of growth remain ongoing narratives destined to unfurl further. Forge ahead with unswerving determination, an open heart, and an unwavering commitment to greatness. Your journey is a testament to your fortitude, resolve, and the limitless potential that beckons on the horizon.